Art Work

Art Work

Poems by

Terry Allen

Cover design by Shay Culligan

ISBN: 978-1-954353-10-7

Kelsay Books
502 South 1040 East, A-119
American Fork, Utah, 84003

Acknowledgments

The author is grateful to the editors of the following journals, where these poems first appeared, some in earlier versions:

Ancient Paths Literary Magazine: "A Brief Encounter" (Reprint)

Bop Dead City: "We Stood on the Fantail and Talked Quietly"

Cloudbank: "Happy Endings"

Constellations: "At the Theatre With My Ten-Year-Old Son"

Dime Show Review: "The Old Man"

Down in the Dirt: "Crapshoot: The Revelation Begins," "Impossible Standards," "Always Nice to Meet a Fan"

Freshwater: "1927"

Into the Void: "The Rule of Three"

Steam Ticket: A Third Coast Review: "Isadora"

Third Wednesday: "Lawn Ornaments Try Positive Thinking," "Latin," "Still in His Cups, Bacchus Looked Down From Mount Olympus and Laughed," "To Quote Miss Betsey Trotwood: *Donkeys!*," "Jacob Marley," "Pull the Other One," "Two Old Friends on Their Early Morning Constitutional"

Well Versed: "Origami Cranes," The Healing Drum," "Later," "A Brief Encounter," "Haiku Hiding in the Dark," "Walking Toward the Edge of the World to See the Elephant," "The Last Reel," "Sunday, December 24, 1944," "Long Ago in the Dreamtime"

Whirlwind Magazine: "The Queen of the Southern Seas Waits and Watches"

Contents

Haiku Hiding in the Dark

In long deep shadows
old keys strike ghostly pages—
pecking out lost lives.

I

Isadora

Born Angela Isadora Duncan,
a Gemini raised in genteel poverty,
she began dancing as a child
until one day she sailed away
on a cattle boat to England
and became the most famous
dancer in the world.

> *Goodbye America,*
> *I shall never see you again,*
> she would say,

as she danced to her own muse,
danced barefoot
in thin see-through clothing
danced with complete freedom of movement,
scantily clad as a woodland nymph
or dressed in long white tunics,
wanting people to see her body
as she skipped, jumped
and ran across the stage.

> *My motto is: no limits,*
> she would say,

while living an eccentric bohemian life,
sometimes labeled a feminist or Darwinist
or communist . . . oh my.

> *Don't let them tame you,*
> she would say,

as she lived out loud by her own rules,
dancing free and natural
like waves in the ocean
like trees swaying in the wind,

until one day her enormous red silk scarf
blew into the well of the rear wheel
of a brand-new 1927 convertible sports car
and wound around the axle,
tightening about Isadora's neck
and dragging her from the car
onto the cobblestone street.

She died instantly,
but because some told her she couldn't
and others told her she shouldn't,
Isadora dances at night
in the moonlight still,
barefoot with the angels
on the head of a pin
or on anything else
she damn well pleases.

Within us lurks the breaker of all laws,
she liked to say.

Pull the Other One

If the ancient Greeks
developed tragedy
on a dreary Monday morning,
then by Friday afternoon,
after the factory whistle
blew, they developed
comedy, just for a little
relief. After all, tragedies
dealt with the big themes
of pride and loss,
often with bodies
piling up by the time
the last lines were spoken,
but the comedies . . .
the comedies were . . .
well funny. They
mocked men in power
for the fools that they were,
and they could get away
with ridiculing absolute
monarchs. They could tell
the truth and utter words
of wisdom because
they were not taken seriously.
They were the royal buffoons
in baggy pants, swinging
rubber chickens
and using them for several
good phallus jokes,
after all, theatre in ancient
Greece was performed
to honor Dionysus,
the god of wine and fertility

and so, a good comedy
could sneak up on
authority and pull
its pants down
or give it a good wedgie.
It's like Bertolt Brecht
said . . . one
shouldn't fight
dictators, one should
ridicule them . . .
but then again,
perhaps, the Greeks
understood that we
should do both.

Still in His Cups, Bacchus Looked Down from Mount Olympus and Laughed

Gazing across the Rubicon,
Julius Caesar spoke in Greek
not Latin
when he said
Let the die be cast,
and even then
it was mistranslated,
but no matter.
It was something he liked
to say, and he would repeat
himself often
much to the annoyance
of those around him.
It was a sentiment
he'd borrowed
from the Greek playwright
Menander who wrote
domestic comedies
about boy meets girl,
boy likes girl,
girl likes boy
parents don't like
boy and girl together
and from that point on,
you guessed it,
obstacles are placed
in their path
until finally
all the obstacles

are removed and . . .
so forth and so forth . . .
and so forth . . .
until they finally
are allowed to wed.
Pretty funny stuff.
And from those comedies,
Julius Caesar would come away
laughing and repeating
Menander's lines
often enough
that friends would wager,
when they got together
at a party,
how long it would take him
to drop the one
about games beginning
and dies being cast,
just as the wine was served
and when he did
everyone would laugh,
me included,
and that's when my friend Aurelia
who didn't see what was so funny
would poke me in the ribs
and say, *Whom the gods love dies young,*
quoting Menander.

Name that Dog

It was a time when I would drive
my son to elementary school,
and we would tune in to the jazz
station out of Minneapolis
and hear Anita O'Day singing,
Pick yourself up, dust yourself off,
and he would say, *That's from "Swing Time"*
and I would feel the same sort of pride
other parents must have felt when they told
their neighbors and anyone else who
would listen that their second-grader
was a straight-A student.

That's right, I would say. *It's from*
"Swing Time," and we would talk about
Fred Astaire and Ginger Rogers
until we finally slipped into one
of our favorite games: Name That Dog!

What's the name of Nick and Nora's pet
wire fox terrier in "The Thin Man?" I'd say.

Asta. What's the name of the dog
in "The Uninvited?" he'd ask.

Ralph, I'd say with a straight face.

No. It's Bobby. Don't you remember him
chasing a squirrel inside that empty house
and then being afraid to go up the stairs
because of the ghosts?

That's right, I'd say. *What about the dog*
in "The Wizard of Oz?"

Toto, of course. Everyone knows that.

Well, what was the name of the dog
that played Toto?

Terry the terrier!

By that time, we'd have arrived
at his school and I'd drop him off
and I'd recall on the way to work
a time when we were at the public
library in the media section, looking
at films to borrow, when a lady
close by yanked a boy about my son's age
by the arm and pulled him away
saying, *No, that's not for you.*
Over here, these are the children's movies.
And we looked to see what the boy
had picked up and it was Charlie Chaplin
in "Modern Times."

I think he would have liked that one,
my son said.

Daltons, 1892

The five boys were a bit overconfident
when they planned
that daylight robbery in Kansas.

Let's hit two Coffeyville banks
at the same time and make us
some outlaw history, they said,

which sounded like a good idea.
After all, who was going to stop 'em?
They'd spent the last year and a half

terrorizing Oklahoma and robbing
a bunch of trains, although truth told
they'd really had more murders than loot

to their credit. Anyway, that day
they rode into town and hitched
their horses to a fence in an alley

near the banks and split up
which wasn't much of a good idea
and it was while stuffing

all that money into grain sacks
that the townspeople ran for their guns
and started blasting the boys

through the bank windows
and whenever and wherever
they poked their heads

out of one door or the other
and that's when the gang fled
down that same back alley

where they had their horses
and were immediately shot
and killed, 'cept for Emmett,

but the boys did manage to take
four townspeople with 'em.
Emmett received twenty-three gunshot wounds

and served fourteen years
of a life sentence in prison
then leveraged his fame

as a former Wild West bandit
and became a Hollywood screenwriter.
He even wrote himself a film

called *When the Daltons Rode*
a tall tale with not much truth
to it starring Randolph Scott

and Kay Francis
with Andy Devine
thrown in for comic effect.

As for Emmett, he died
several years after moving
to California at the age of sixty-six in 1937.

That might be the finish of the story,
but there's an epilogue that should
be tacked on to kind of round

everything out and put a period
on it. You see, the boys
were trying to get away

from those banks in Coffeyville
with only a few thousand dollars
stuffed in grain sacks,

which is really chicken feed today
when it comes to bank robbery,
and that just goes to show how times

change on us all. For instance,
in Kansas today, they got a bunch
of Wells Fargo banks,

the ones with the six-horse stagecoach
riding through the Wild West,
which the bank says is a symbol

of the company's heritage:
service, stability and innovation.
So, don't start laughing when I

tell you that just this year Wells Fargo
had to pay one billion dollars to settle
lending abuses that the executives

and board of directors were responsible for,
which is only about two to two and a half percent
of the banks' net income in one year,

which makes some folks think
that Emmett might be rolling over
in his grave because he's itching

to write *that* screenplay, with a whole lot
of funny actors in it for comic effect.

Always Nice to Meet a Fan

I recall now and then
the construction worker
I met on the Staten Island Ferry
early one evening.

He appeared to be heading
home from work while I
was on a joyride to take
in the majestic view
of the New York Harbor,
the Statue of Liberty,
and Ellis Island,
where European immigrants
on my father's side first
arrived in America,
while my mother and I
entered through San Francisco
many years later
as immigrants from Australia.

He was a rough, husky man,
wearing well-worn, steel-toed
work boots, safety vest,
hard hat and had a green Stanley
lunch box and thermos at his feet.

In my ignorance, I felt I knew
this man and would have
no surprise at what he might say
and that's when he opened his lunch box
and took out a book on ballet,
with a colorful cover
that pictured dancers
in leotards and tutus

caught for an instant
in acrobatic flight.

As he was reading, I struck up
a conversation and asked him
about his interest in ballet
and was told that he didn't
know that much about it yet,
but he felt he needed to learn
since his real passion
was opera, and so he'd checked
out a book from the library
to get started and that led
him to talking about
Beverly Sills who had
announced her retirement
and would be giving her
final singing performance
in her Farewell Gala
at New York City Opera,
where he was hoping to get
a ticket when they went
on sale to the public.

That sounds wonderful, I said.

Oh yes, he said, looking
up at the clouds floating by
and listening for something
that I could not hear.

She has a voice that can slice
through the largest orchestra
and chorus. A voice like no other.
She's a lyric coloratura, he said.

I like to think that he had the best
seat in the house for Beverly Sills'
farewell performance.

Over the River and Down the Rabbit Hole

My first thesis advisor
in graduate school
was like the Black Knight
in a Monty Python movie
who guards the one bridge
from here to there
with a stern warning
that *None shall pass!*
The problem for me
was that as a theatre
professor with an emphasis
in early history, literature
and criticism, he was
suspicious of anything
written after 1650
and hostile to anything
written in the twentieth
century and there I was,
proposing to examine
a modern playwright
whose first play
was written and produced
only eleven years earlier.

Who is this mysterious character?
My advisor would ask. *Who*
does he work for? What does
he want?

We're not told, I would say.

What? Doesn't the writer
tell us? Doesn't he know?

I think if we asked him,
he would say, "I don't know.
My characters tell me so much
and no more. I just write
what they say and follow the clues."

Hasn't he written notes
or a biography of each
of his characters,
outlining their historical,
physiological, sociological,
and psychological makeup?

He says that's not how he
experiences the world.
People don't come up to him
and hand him their resume
before they speak.

Nonsense. That's absurd.

Well, yes, it is.
Theatre of the Absurd,
to be precise.

And in my mind today,
I can still hear my thesis
advisor say, in the voice
of the Black Knight
I move for no Man!

Although, now that I think
about it, he may have been
more like the Doorknob

at the end of the rabbit hole
who tells Alice
that the way through
is *Simply Impassible.*

At the Theatre with My Ten-Year-Old Son

He was the only child in the audience
that night and many patrons
looked at me as if I had brought
an ocelot into the theatre.
What is that? I thought I heard
a woman ask her husband,
as the lights faded, and she
leaned forward in her seat
to get a better look. *Hush,*
he seemed to reassure her,
It's just a large cat.

But once the play began,
which was about two tramps
passing time as they waited for Godot,
who never came by the end of Act I
and never came a second time
by the end of Act II, we were forgotten.

I remember that much of the audience
seemed confused by the play
and some frustrated few were ready to yell
an *Amen!* in agreement with an early critic
who said that Mr. Becket had succeeded
in writing a play that means nothing.

But children are different.
They get what they get
and for the most part
don't worry about the rest.

And so, once it was over
and the actors took their bows
and the house lights came up

and the audience moved from their seats
into the aisles and shuffled out to their cars,
and their lives and their cats and their dogs,
we sat and talked and being the oh-so-wise
adult, I said, *Here's a good question:*
If there was a third act to this play,
what do you think would happen?

I asked him in full confidence,
certain that my ten-year-old had seen
the pattern and would know
that the two tramps, Didi and Gogo,
would wait endlessly day after day,
passing time as best they could
as they waited for Godot
to come to bring meaning
to their lives, but instead without a beat
his answer came back, full of confidence
and certainty, *I think they'd give up,*
move to town and start a circus.

And as we talked of Didi and Gogo
as sad face tramps under the big top,
a stagehand brought out
a single bare light bulb on a stand
and placed it down center on the stage.
What's that for? my son asked.

That's the ghost light, I said.
It keeps the theatre ghosts company
and helps them see in the dark,
so they don't knock over furniture
and cause accidents.

It's a night light, he said
as we got up from our seats.

Yes, I said.

While they're waiting . . .
my son said as we walked
up the aisle and out into the night.

To Quote Miss Betsey Trotwood: *Donkeys!*

He was a funny kid in high school. Not odd. Funny. Although he did like to read *Soldier of Fortune* magazine. Still, he had a certain charm. He was playful, and he had a keen sense of humor, which has nothing to do with being able to laugh at other people's jokes. It has to do with being able to write the jokes, which also has to do with comic timing. In other words, he was perfectly cast as any one of Shakespeare's fools . . . maybe Dogberry in *Much Ado About Nothing* or Nick Bottom in *A Midsummer's Night Dream* or one of the Gravediggers in *Hamlet.* In fact, I once did cast him as Grumio in *The Taming of the Shrew,* and he was great in rehearsals as Petruchio's all-too-clever manservant who used his wits to outdo people of higher social standing until he informed me before one rehearsal that he would not be able to do the role because his parents objected to one of his lines where Grumio refers to a half-witted suitor in the play as an "ass," and it really did no good to explain that the word did not mean someone's backside, but was speaking of an animal . . . meaning an extremely stupid or foolish person, like the word asinine derived from the Latin *asinus,* meaning ass or donkey. But that was that. He didn't do the role once his parents said that it didn't matter what the word meant. It only mattered what some people thought it meant. I've wondered from time to time what happened to him. The last I knew, he was torn in his ambition to either become a missionary or a mercenary.

Jacob Marley

Performed by a local character actor
who specializes in playing
the wrinkled and the dead
and directed by our postmistress
who is known for her scenes
of spectacular crowd control
and soaring language,
sung more than spoken,
by actors who alarmingly
cross down center
and intone their lines directly
to the audience with grand leaps
of vocal gymnastics,
the character of poor Jacob Marley
is there before us to frighten Scrooge
and the children in the audience
with strange moans,
contorted facial expressions
punctuated by the rattling of chains,
without the slightest bit
of understand as to why
he is haunting his old partner
seven years after his death,
except to say that Scrooge
will be visited by three spirits
which for the audience
is enough, never mind
that the lines have been drastically cut
to bring the production in under
sixty minutes, lest the audience's
attention is strained,

never mind that we never quite
learn that the common welfare
of mankind is the business of everyone,
never mind that Marley fails to tell us
that charity, mercy, forbearance
and benevolence should be the business
of Ebenezer Scrooge and the business
of each one of us
sitting in the dark auditorium
and when the play is over
and Tiny Tim asks for God's blessing,
the audience leaps to its feet
and the woman next to me
asks above the roar of the crowd,
how did they learn all those lines?

A Brief Encounter

Imagine you are asked
to describe Ebenezer Scrooge
by a space alien from one
of the seventeen billion earth-sized
planets in our galaxy for some reason
that seems very important to him.
Naturally, you want to be helpful
because you remember the time
you got lost in Cleveland

and so how do you respond
to the alien? How do you get to the heart
of the matter? Do you say
if anyone knows how to keep
Christmas well, it's Ebenezer Scrooge,
and then quickly add that you'll
explain Christmas later. Do you
say that Scrooge was as good
a man as this world ever knew,

and that if people laughed at his high
spirits, generosity and good cheer
that he was wise enough to know
that nothing ever happens in this world
for good at which some people do not
have their fill of laughter

or do you answer the alien's
question by reaching into a worn
bag of tired bits and pieces and pull out
a handful of words like *tightfisted, cold,*
covetous old sinner,

and if you do, might you not
be surprised that the visitor
shakes his head and turns away

and somehow you know
at that moment
that he'll return home and report
that he visited a world
where its inhabitants
don't yet understand
or believe in redemption.

Walking Toward the Edge of the World to See the Elephant

He had thought that as long
as there were children
there would be circuses
and clowns, but now
it was shutting down
after 146 years . . .

all gone . . .
the white face clowns,
the sad face tramps . . .
All. Gone.

He had been part
of the Greatest Show on Earth:

the clown cars,
sweet cotton candy,
midnight train whistles.
triple-time bass bands,
old-time calliopes,

and there were the crowds
and the dancing bears,
and all those balloons.

Now he hasn't put
his make-up on for months.

First, attendance dropped
and the elephants were retired
and then there were reports
of threatening clowns
popping up all around the country.

The New Orleans District
Attorney Jim Garrison
once said that someday there
would even be a book written
that blames JFK's assassination
on "retired circus clowns."

You know when a clown retires?
He thinks as he walks further
on toward the edge of the world.
It's when he dies . . .

or when he's shot
with a water canon
and does a double flip
backwards and a daisy
pops out of his chest!

The Last Reel

That's life. Whichever way you turn, Fate sticks out a foot to trip you.
—Al Robert in Detour (1945)

in the lightless corner
of a dim room
in a landscape
in black and white
with eyes open
he slides down the wall
as thoughts blur
like fog creeping
over black water
why . . . ?
he says in a faint voice
that trails off in a wet
guttural gasp

in the dark
crushed cigarette
smoke rises

and moonlight flickers
through broken glass
and venetian blinds

as she steps out
of the shadows
with a small gun

a spider in satin
with pearls
and lace

her with a past
and he
with no future

II

1910

In September's light the Vatican introduced
a compulsory oath against Modernism
to be taken by all priests upon ordination.

The world was changing and the artist
was recast as a revolutionary
like those wicked French Impressionists
who rejected simple realism
in favor of a style interested
in the quality of color, light
and the time of day.

These artists left the studio
and painted outdoors
to capture a single moment,
they said.

Some American painters,
like Daniel Garber, were inspired
by the French Impressionist style
in his luminous, poetic renditions
of the Delaware River near his home
in Buck's County, Pennsylvania.

Far from Rome and Paris in 1910,
he painted the transient effects
of light and atmosphere
in landscapes with quick brush strokes
of broken color creating a tapestry-like quality
suggesting the effects of flickering light
across the water and riverbank.

His was a fresh, spontaneous style
of vibrant color, although by the 1930s
the world had changed again
and his impressionist style was regarded
as old-fashioned by critics.

In 1958, he fell off a ladder
in his studio and died.
By 1967 the Vatican rescinded
its compulsory oath against Modernism
when it no longer mattered.

1927

Alright, Mr. DeMille, I'm ready for my close-up.
—Norma Desmond in Sunset Boulevard

With only thirty-seven million casualties,
the war to end wars is over.
Yeats warns that the center cannot hold
and the Fitzgeralds are in Paris.

The Jazz Age is in full swing
and prohibition is the law
of the land at home
and damn is it profitable.
Al Capone earns sixty million dollars
by year's end from alcohol sales alone.

Louis Armstrong cuts his first recording
and Duke Ellington settles in as pianist
and bandleader at the Cotton Club,
while Al Jolson sings and speaks
in the first talkie,
which will prove to be the ruin
of some silent film stars like Norma Desmond.

Flappers go out to all night parties
without a man
to look after them.
They drive fast cars,
smoke in public,
drink booze,
wear makeup
and hold men's hands
without wearing gloves.

They dance the Charleston,
the Shimmy and . . . oh my . . . the Black Bottom
dances that fit
their fast-paced lifestyle.

As the world's population
reaches 3 billion
and a post-war generation
clings to youth as if it could be
taken from them at any moment,
the center cannot hold
and all is expanding.

And yet in a quiet New York studio,
Georgia O'Keeffe fills a large canvas
with two giant red and orange poppies
with deep purple centers,
so inviting and dark
that one can almost
fall into them.

The Rule of Three

Three elderly professors examine a large painting in an art gallery.

There's the Holy Trinity of course.
Oh my, yes.
Omne trium perfectum.
It gives one pause just to think on it.

Friends, Romans and Countrymen.
Simple, appealing . . .
And effective.
We're pattern-seeking machines.
No doubt.
Oh yes.

Entertainment?
Hope, Crosby, and Lamour.
Patty, Maxene, and LaVerne.
Groucho, Harpo, and Chico.
Larry, Curly, and Moe.
Not to take things too lightly.
Oh no.

Some primitive cultures . . .
Yes?
Famously had only the numbers one, two, and many.
Really?
Oh yes.

But why three oranges?
Ah! That's the great mystery.
Why not for instance . . . no oranges at all?
No oranges?
Yes.
You may have touched on something there.
Yes?

No oranges and yet the piece is titled “Interior with Three
  Oranges.”
Oh my.

The viewer would then need to . . .
Yes?
Have faith that the oranges are there nonetheless.
Hidden perhaps.
Out of view.
But notwithstanding . . .
They are present.
Just beyond the frame.
Out of reach.
Oh my.
Yes.

But what if nothing were outside the frame?
So, there is no outside?
The frame contains everything.
Everything visible perhaps?
Even the dark matter.
Composed of some as-yet undiscovered subatomic particles.

Leaving us feeling a bit cold.
A bit out of place.
A bit unmoored.

Oh yes.

Lawn Ornaments Try Positive Thinking

The state of your life is nothing more than a reflection of your state of mind.
—Wayne Dyer

You do not have to be defeated by anything.
You do not have to stay frozen with inaction
and allow the world to simply move around you.

You only have to want peace of mind,
improved health and a never-ceasing
flow of energy. It's all up to you.
You must decide to end inertia,

throw open a window
and go for all the confidence,
success and joy
to which you are entitled.

So what if you're pink
and stand on one leg all day?
How many among us can sustain
such divine stillness?

Let others ridicule and poison
themselves with negative energy.
You must refuse to hear,
speak or see all evil within or without.
Put all such thoughts farthest from your mind.

Say it loud and proud, *I have metal jiggle wings!*
Say, *I have lavender wind spinners!*
Say, *I'm a garden cow and proud of it!*

Say, *I am a wild chicken wobbler!*
Do you think that's easy?
You have a springed head and tail, for god's sake.
You make people laugh. That's no small thing.

So all you metal birds, bugs and lawn art;
all you flying pigs, kissing frogs,
rain snails, and celestial cherubs,
stand tall . . . or squat tall!
Be proud! Celebrate! You are shiny, artistic,
understated and sophisticated.

Like the least among us,
you can do all that He has done,
and more.

Latin

Maybe I should learn Latin, then I could read Cicero or Virgil or Julius Caesar's *The Conquest of Gaul* the way they were meant to be read and I'd come to understand things like the plural of memorandum is memoranda and I'd know why a male graduate is an alumnus and a female graduate an alumna. Or maybe I could just become a better Catholic. It's been said that the Devil hates Latin, because it's the universal language of the church. After all, Pope Benedict announced his resignation in Latin; however, there were a whole lot of cardinals that didn't know what the hell he was saying. If I were fluent in Latin and I were a cardinal, I'd be the head of my class. But then again, most cardinals spend at least two years studying at one of the universities in Rome. I don't think I'm up to learning two languages, even though I'm told that my brain's neuroplasticity keeps decreasing with age, and so I have to use it or lose it and since I'm not interested in crossword puzzles, Sudoku or Trivial Pursuit, I may have to keep my brain nimble by learning Latin, which would be very helpful if I wanted to become a doctor, although I may not be up to the four years of undergraduate school, four years of medical school and three to seven years of residency training just to keep my brain nimble. But still, with a command of Latin, I'd surely be able to protect myself from demonic forces and maybe, just like Harry Potter and Professor Severus Snape, use difficult spells like *expecto patronum* to protect against dementors and I'm thinking that if I could do that, I could use Latin spells to fight off psychic vampires, like televangelists or pharmaceutical executives, who feed off the life force of other living creatures. Oh well. Never mind. I'm getting tired now. Maybe I *could* play Trivial Pursuit. I already know that the capital of Delaware is Dover and that the King Cobra is the world's longest venomous snake.

Happy Endings

The Smithsonian has announced the 60 finalists of its Annual Photo Contest, selected from 48,000 submissions, which makes my mind turn to Mathew Brady, one of the earliest photographers in American history, best known for his images of the Civil War. What many don't recall is that following the conflict, a war-weary public lost interest in seeing photos of the war, and Brady's popularity declined, and he declared bankruptcy and died penniless in the charity ward of Presbyterian Hospital in New York City from complications after a streetcar accident. Which just goes to show that Orson Welles may have been right when he said, a century later, that *there are no happy endings if the rest of the story is told.* Why even the first printed version of Little Red Riding Hood ends when the wolf, having eaten grandmother, tricks Red into climbing in bed with him and then eats her, too. The end. No hunter. No woodsman to save the day. No being swallowed whole like Jonah in the whale or Saint Margaret in the dragon, only to reemerge unharmed. No teeth marks. No snipping the wolf open to find both granny and Red very much alive. Not at all. In fact, I like to think that there was a popular riddle posed to children at the time the first version of the story was written down in the seventeenth century: How did the wolf eat Little Red Riding Hood and her grandmother? And the answer, of course, would be: One big awful bite at a time. And even if Little Red does somehow escape the wolf and end up living happily ever after as later versions tell the tale with an added warning not to talk to strangers in the woods . . . if the rest of the story is told . . . Red is probably going to be struck by a streetcar and die in a charity ward anyway.

Two Old Friends on Their Early Morning Constitutional

A bit chilly today.
No rain though.
Oh no.
We've had enough of that.
I'd say so.

My word.
What?
Is this new?
I don't believe I've seen it before.
It looks as if it sprang up overnight.
Someone's been busy.

I rather like it.
Do you?
There's something about it.
Well, metal art works can stir the imagination.

It reminds me of my first wife.
Does it?
Yes.
Did I ever meet her? I don't recall.
It was a long time ago.

What was her name?
It doesn't come to me at the moment.
Think of something else. That usually works.

You know, I did a bit of welding when I was younger.
Did you? So did I.
Oh yes. Nothing big. Just puttering about.
It's amazing what people have in common.

It’s the tools that I recall most.
Do you? That’s funny.
There’s the three-inch offset sheet metal bender with forged blades.
Oh my. That takes me back.
And the tinner’s hammer with shock reduction grip.
And the good ol’ duct ripper.

You treat them right and they treat you right.
They’ll never let you down.
Do you recall the dogleg reamer?
Oh yes and what about the stork beak pliers?

Did you ever see a spud wrench?
I did.
Well, I had two.
Really?

Oh my. Oh my.
The memories.

Helen.

Origami Cranes

They married in a glass house.

She in dove white.
He in cement gray.
She in peep-toed pumps.
He in orange sneakers.

She began planning
her wedding
in grade three.
And now it was
coming true
in the refracted light
of the green house.

And for a moment,
as a poem was read,
as a song was sung,
as the pastor spoke,
she thought ahead
to the colorful folded cranes
the guests would find
scattered across each table
at the reception.

Vows were said.
Promises made
to love, honor, and cherish
'til death do us part. Yet
at that moment,
when those words
were spoken
and smiles were fixed,
and eyes were moist

and cheeks were flushed
not a thought
was given

to the fact
if all went well
and the luck
of one thousand origami cranes
held true and
God's loving grace
was present in their lives,
that one of the two
would indeed
bury the other.

New Year's Eve

If Tweedledum or Tweedledee made a New Year's resolution, someone asks, what would it be? And that's when you jump in because you've been thinking about this question for some time. They'd join a health club and try to shed a few pounds, you say. With all that bouncing about and honking, it's got to be hard on the joints and if they're smart, they could check to see if their insurance includes Silver Sneakers. They'd certainly qualify age-wise. They've got to be almost 150 years old, if we're talking about Lewis Carroll's version of the fat twin brothers in *Through the Looking Glass and What Alice Found There.* Although it's possible you're thinking of James Joyce's characterization of Sigmund Freud and Carl Gustav Jung as the Tweedle brothers but that would be another story or maybe it's the opening song "Tweedle Dee & Tweedle Dum" on Bob Dylan's 2001 album *Love And Theft* that you have in mind, but no matter which, I still think a membership in a health club would suit them best and perhaps with good healthy exercise they would temper their aggressive tendencies and not battle quite as much over things of little or no importance.

Thinking of Ireland While in the Dentist's Chair Waiting for the Novocaine to Do Its Thing

And why not? Ireland was the home
of Brendan Behan, one of the greatest Irish
hell-raisers, talkers and writers of all time,
who as a boy was first set off on poetry
and the love of language by Sister Monica,
the head of the North William Street School
in Dublin where he grew up to become
a celebrated drunk who, even pissed to the gills,
never once stooped to the use of a frivolous
ampersand in a moment of weakness
while writing his poems in the Irish,
as they say, and he was a boyo who never ever
scattered his words over a blank page
like so many feral pigeon droppings atop
the Fusiliers' Arch on St Stephen's Green
and I can see him now in my mind's eye
raising a pint in Davy Byrne's Pub
and I can hear him singing *God Save Ireland*
just as I begin to doze and a bit of drool
rolls down my left cheek as I try
my best to raise my voice with the ghosts
about me, *God save Ireland, said they all.*

What Do You Do When You're Asked to Write About a Scottish Poet Who Was Asked to Write About a Tool or Utensil?

Maybe you could focus on the tool and write about a pocket knife. After all, you've been carrying one since you were a scout. They're great tools. Everyone should have one, but be mindful that it doesn't help when you're going through airport security in Bangkok, Singapore or Dubai to insist that according to the Second Amendment to the United States Constitution, American citizens have the right to bear arms. In fact, it might be a good idea to not bring up that American citizen stuff at all in those situations. So, if you don't write about a pocket knife because of thorny international laws, maybe you could write about that restaurant-quality spatula that you bought at an estate sale or what about that electric razor you use every morning? Or . . . wait a minute . . . maybe you could skip the tool prompt and hone in on the idea that the poet is Scottish and write about those nineteen- and twenty-year-old American college students who study abroad for a semester in Edinburgh but have no interest in Scottish poetry or any poetry . . . students who, it turns out, only have three interests: the first being travel, which is helped in that all weekends are three-day weekends in their study aboard program, except for those four-day weekends that are bank holidays and that allows those American students to travel every weekend, not in Scotland . . . they're already there for god's sake . . . but to the many pubs in London, the beer gardens in Munich and the bars in Amsterdam, which tells you that their second big interest in studying abroad is drinking which leads inevitably to their third interest which is karaoke. So, it'll only fall on deaf ears if you bring up Scottish poets like Robert Burns who said it would be a wonderful gift if we could see ourselves as others see us.

So, it might be best to write about that electric razor after all. It has 40,000 cross-cutting actions, two specialized middle trimmers, two ultra-thin optifoils, one dedicated skin guard, and it's designed to shave the trickiest of hair smoothly. Plus, it's made in Germany. So, it's like taking a trip to Europe every morning without going through airport security, or learning a new language . . . or learning anything at all.

The Past

Poets are writing a lot these days about going back in time
and meeting their parents when they were young.

I try not to be too hard on them, she says.

He says, *I give them a good talking to.*

I know what you mean, she says. *In my mind,*
they always seem so smug about the future . . .
far too optimistic.

Like the world owes them happiness, he says.

I tell them that I wouldn't have turned out
so messed up if they had tried harder.

I would have liked to have had different parents . . .
ones that were more adventurous and creative
. . . maybe a world-famous botanist who explores
tropical rainforests for plant life that leads to the cure
of deadly diseases and another one who
is a great tenor or soprano at the Metropolitan Opera.

They always end up looking stunned when I
hand them a list of my grievances. I tell them
don't you look at me in that tone of voice.

Like they don't know there's room for improvement.

Exactly.

The poets sit in silence and sip their lattes as they make
a few notes on their yellow legal pads.
The coffee shop is quiet with only the mournful sounds
of Chet Baker's trumpet in the background
playing "Alone Together."

Oh, here's a good one, she says, as she circles
an item in her dog-eared copy of the March/April issue
of *Poets and Writers* magazine.

What's that? he says, as he finishes the last bite
of his blackberry-lemon scone.

*Red Squirrel Review is looking for brilliant submissions
on the subject of reinventing the past.*

I already have an idea, he says.

Me, too, she says.

Long Ago in the Dreamtime

When the animals were the first on the earth,
when there was only a moon and stars above,
the beautiful dancing bird stole
the emu's large egg and threw it
into the sky. It landed on stacked firewood,
spilling its yellow yolk that burst into flames,
painting the clouds in red ochre
and lighting the world below
and the kookaburra laughed to awaken
all to greet the Sun Woman,
the bringer of life and warmth.

III

The Old Man

The old man, asleep perhaps
on a tired bench,
slumps forward
and a torn bit of paper
slips from his fingers and falls
to the ground,
dancing for a moment
in a cool breeze,
as an edgy piano plays

twelve-bar blues

from a club, a block
or two down a well-worn street,
as the ragged edges of the city
curl and fold into itself.

The Healing Drum

I look at the healing drum
atop a shelf in the darkened hallway.
Silent now,
it whispers still of life's evolving journey
if only through the spiral symbol
at the center of its head.

Oh, how you liked fireworks
on the Fourth of July,
not the showy floral displays
painted across the night sky,
but the booms that barked
and bounced off banks and parked cars.
Those blasts, you said, went straight to your soul.

You laughed with joy then,
just as you did when listening for fifteen minutes
to the *1812 Overture,* in anticipation
of the climactic volley of rhythmic cannon fire,
ringing chimes and brass fanfares of its finale.

Studies say that loneliness can be deadlier than obesity.
Maybe so.
If we can be merciful even with ourselves, you said,
we might come to know
that being a good person is all that matters.
And yet,
the only time your eyes filled with tears
was when you said, *I hope I've been good enough.*

It is said that the spiral helps consciousness accept
the turnings and changes of life as it evolves.
Maybe so.
But all I see when I turn my head from the drum
to the window
is a clear blank sky and the green and yellow
recycling barrel at the end of the driveway,
tilted to one side,
one if its wheels off, yet again.

I reach out and touch the healing drum on the shelf,
tracing the spiral from the inside out.

Puffs of Wind

"Tiny, rapid puffs of wind. There is no sound attached to them."
—Robert Lanza with Bob Berman, Biocentrism

Driving south
on Highway 86
along the flats
between the Salton Sea
and Santa Rosa Mountains,

the smell of fertilizer
and fresh vegetables
hangs in the cold
night, desert air.

The hypnotic buzz of tires
along a broken white line
counterpoints off the beat
to the insistent thumping
of a distant radio station,

when a competing voice,
breaking up,
crackles through:

The devil . . . let a man
stop to think . . .
go fast now . . .
can't see me for dust . . .

These fevered words
overpowered now
by George Jones
and Tammy Wynette
and I listen
as I watch the strange

radiant desert
revealed in the truck's
headlights:
a landscape covered
in sagebrush and scrub,
with the odd Joshua tree,
reaching its hands
to heaven in prayer.

. . . then thou scarest me
with dreams,
and terrifiest me
through visions . . .

And George and Tammy's voices
break through again,
clear as a West Virginia
church bell on a Sunday morning:

Rollin' in my sweet baby's arms
Rollin' in my sweet baby's arms

Oh yeah!
I keep time
on the steering wheel
with my thumb.

Rollin' in my sweet baby's arms

There is so much life
rolling around in the desert
that I can’t see,
although the sun
is just beginning to tint
the horizon

and there, for a moment,
beyond the cracked windshield,
laid out before me,
is the moon, the Milky Way,
a shooting star
and the impending dawn.

And for a moment, it’s 1962,
August the fifth,
the first quasar
is located by radio
and I’m behind the wheel,
of a surf green 1957 Chevy,
a sixteen-year-old
listening to a voice
that says Marilyn Monroe
was found dead
and I watch as three red roses
drop their petals.

Rollin’ in my sweet baby’s arms

And the truck lurches a bit
and my thoughts leap
to the meteor impact
that changed the biosphere
65 million years ago

and I think of the house
where I grew up
that is abandoned now
to raccoons,
a house that was once alive
with the comings and goings
of a family that planned
to live there forever.

What did Lazarus see when he
was dead for four days?
Does the mind die
with the body?

Time to pull off the road
for coffee at a local cafe,
if one can be found.

And for a moment,
I imagine turning
off the highway
and into the year 1942
and pulling to a stop
in a dirt parking lot
beside an abandoned street car
which has been converted
into a diner,
and there sits Veronica Lake
at the counter,
all four foot eleven inches
of her, and she smiles
and offers to buy me
the best ham and eggs
and hot Joe in the whole world.

I swerve to avoid
a man in a wet suit
and crumpled fedora
standing on the edge
of the highway
and I seem to hear him
calling after me as I pass,
warning that a mysterious force,
can put the finger
on any one of us
for no good reason at all.

Superstition Mountain lies ahead,
with its live bombing area,
posted for people to keep away.

They should, too.
Naval planes fly overhead,
and drop bombs,
turning plants, animals,
rocks and Joshua trees
into dust.

Apaches believe that the hole
leading down into hell
is located in the Superstitions
and winds blow
from the hole
forming dust devils.

Many years from now,
when this celestial night
is one small flicker
in human history
and the lights finally
do go out,
a tree will fall in the forest
and it won't make a sound.
Limbs, branches and trunk
will violently strike the ground
creating rapid pulses of air,
traveling at 750 mph,
but no one will be there to hear.

Tectonic Shifts

Crippled with arthritis, nearly blind,
the old man stands still,
held upright in the crowd.
A singer screams
each syllable,
each word,
each line,
each verse
with the pounding intensity
of hammers on sheet metal,
her vocal gymnastics
on display as she belts out Dylan
with such ferocity
that the cold, amplified words
shatter as they slam into
an enormous crowd who want to believe
that the times are changing.

But the words don't hold together
in the piercing squall
and his mind drifts
to a concert
somewhere in New York State
fifty-five years ago,
the day after Kennedy was shot,
the day that Dylan opened with a new song
that he had recorded a month earlier,
inspired by Irish and Scottish ballads,
with words that made the old man believe then
that the world was changing
and indeed, it did.

The High-Note Man

Children are more likely to see ghosts, they say
while they play with their toys alone in their rooms
or lie awake in their beds on a moonless night,
that's when they might see a sad little girl with red eyes
staring out of a closet who disappears from sight
when their mom or dad comes in and turns on a light,
or they might wake in the dark and find a lonely old woman
they've never seen before sitting on the bed next to them
and when it's too hot to sleep and the stars
have gone out one by one, they might hear the sounds,
the powerful musical sounds coming from somewhere
or nowhere at all. It's him. It's him. The man with the horn.
Sometimes he's seen. Sometimes he's not.
He's the High-Note Man. Now when he comes around,
he looks like some old fool who's lost
and don't know where he's at, but he's
the heart and the soul, he's the High-Note Man.
And the children who aren't afraid anymore
of the dark get up and move about, after all,
it's a perfect chance to dance with the High-Note Man.

An Irresistible Impulse

Saturday Night, October 1959

Otto Preminger's *Anatomy of a Murder*
was my introduction
to the music of Duke Ellington
and Billy Strayhorn
and the beginning of a lifelong
love affair with jazz.

But what I didn't know
at the time was that 1959
was arguably one of the most
important years in all of jazz history.

It was the year that saw
the passing of Lester Young
and Billy Holiday
and the release of four
defining and influential albums:
Miles Davis' introspective
and haunting, *Kind of Blue,*
Dave Brubeck's rhythmic
experimentation, *Time Out,*
the big man with big hands,
Charles Mingus' powerful,
Mingus Ah Um, and the audacious
free jazz of Ornette Coleman's
The Shape of Jazz to Come.

I didn’t understand it all.
I couldn’t hear it all,
but it was like sticking
a toe into the La Brea Tar Pits
and being sucked under
into a world of endless
fascination and reflection
for decades to come.

Fifty Years Later

Saturday Night, October 2009

I asked my granddaughter
who was playing saxophone
in her high school jazz band,
who were the great saxophonists
that she listened to and admired
and I suppose I was expecting to hear
her take on the bestselling jazz album
of all time, Miles Davis' *Kind of Blue*
with Cannonball Adderley on sax,
or maybe thoughts about Stan Getz playing
cool jazz with The Dave Brubeck Quartet
on *Take Five,* or maybe she'd tell me
how much she liked Sonny Rollins,
Lester Young or Coleman Hawkins,
but when she didn't answer at all,
I asked if she was into the sounds
of John Coltrane or Charlie Parker,
and that's when she stopped me with:

I'm not interested. I don't like history,

said in such a way as to put an end
to any further talk on the matter.

Impossible Standards

Impossible standards just make life
difficult, she said, above the buzz
of Spike's birthday bash, trying her best
to be attractive, charming, witty
and memorable in her new scoop neck,
deep magenta, peasant blouse.

It was raining outside and those on the deck
had already retreated into the great room,
careful to bring the bruschetta, canapés,
and smoked eggs with them.

You have to try the pinot noir,
her voice broke above the waves of chatter
and laughter as she held her glass under my nose.
It has wonderful berry overtones.

I'll stick with my beer. Thanks.

Are you two together? the youngish man in the yellow
cashmere sweater asked, glancing at
us as he tried to balance his plate and scotch
whiskey at the same time.

Yes, I said, into my glass.

He nodded and walked away,
as if that confirmed some important
piece of information needed later when detectives
grilled him about where he was last Friday evening.

I watched him through the bottom
of my glass, when she touched my arm,
saying something out of the corner of her mouth
as she somehow still managed to smile
at a couple across the room by the Orchid Cactus.

What was that? I asked,
really trying to listen to Dave Brubeck
and Eugene Wright and their two-chord,
piano-bass vamp on *Take Five*
and thinking to myself that the writing
was already on the wall
and the ceiling
and across the back of the white leather sofa
and down the side of her rich red-blue blouse.

Don't be so judgmental all the time,
she said. *And remember*
what the prophets tell us:
Understand yourself
so you may understand others.

The Queen of the Southern Seas Waits and Watches

on the coast of central Java

mallets beat a percussive skeleton melody
on bronze metal bars
punctuated by gong chimes

bamboo flutes
and double-headed
barrel drums

as a single female vocalist rises
above an insistent male chorus
accompanying ritual dancers

in vibrant batik sarongs

she looks up to watch bird-nest gatherers
descend a sheer cliff face
to an overhung

rickety bamboo
platform thirty feet above
the churning water

awaiting a wave
then leaping out from the sharp rocks
plunging through salt spray

caught for an instant
in the watery updraft
swept beneath the crag

into dank caves
groping in total darkness
reaching to fill bags

with sea swallow nests
careful when going back
not to misjudge the tides

not to fall into
violent sea foam waves slamming
into jagged rocks

not to dishonor
the Queen of the Southern Seas
who waits and watches

Later

Yes, I'm upset with you, she said,
as she pointed a finger in his direction,
singling him out,
never mind that no one else was near.
She turned and moved quickly down the beach,
cutting off the slightest possibility of talk.
Words, dropping behind her:
It will have to wait
'til this weekend.

My god, he thought.
What did I do
or what didn't I do?
What did I say
or fail to say?
I guess I'll have to wait
'til this weekend.

But the weekend never came.

Instead, ocean waters rose. Coastal villages
and towns disappeared. Gamelan orchestras sank
below boiling blue-green waves. Rip currents
pulled bamboo xylophones, drums, gongs and flutes
out to sea. The earth trembled and cracked open. Gaseous clouds,
ash and volcanic bombs hurled into the air.
Giant reptiles crawled out of Tokyo Bay,
breathing fire and trampling heavy-footed through city streets.

Graves opened.
The dead arose and lumbered toward nearby farm houses.

And planet Earth fell into the Sun.

Crapshoot: The Revelation Begins

2012—So long ago

The sample space for an experiment
is the set of all possible outcomes,
the man in the white bathrobe
reassures himself as he sits
quite alone at two a.m.
next to a massive stone fireplace,
in his cozy two-story great room,
unaware that a giant locust
with the tail of a scorpion
crawls across his left shoulder.

While under a blood moon,
an odd clownish man with an origami
comb over studies the report
written on the back of a hotel bar napkin
from someone on his team of private investigators
sent to Hawaii to uncover
one of the greatest cons
in the history of politics and beyond.

At the same time, the four horsemen crouch
beside a stair-stoop on a dark, wet city street.
The pale rider, always the reader,
rolls a pair of orange dice in his hands,
glances at the others and says, *Did you know*
that in Japan, men with comb overs
are called bar code men?

And at that moment, a faint red star
in Alpha Centauri, lets loose
its grip on the universe
and begins to fall from the sky
while a single celestial trumpet
blows some sweet ass blues.

We Stood on the Fantail and Talked Quietly

and watched the receding lights
of the city above the wake of the ship
as it eased out of the harbor
and headed east for her last summer crossing.
The recirculating water churned
behind in a widening V with the air still
and the surface of the lake
smooth as the Queen's dark mirror
reflecting the moon and the stars
with the summer triangle rising
above the northeastern horizon—
the swan, the harp and the eagle
seeming to vibrate to Aretha Franklin
asking for a little respect.

Our summer had been spent
sailing Lake Michigan.
Six hours across. Two hours in port.
Six hours across. Two hours in port.
For three months.
Six hours across. Two hours in port.

We survived, I said.

Yes, you agreed.

But we missed the summer of love,
one of us said.

You're telling me, the other replied.

Sunday, December 24, 1944

Every time the old man listened
to *Silent Night,* it brought him to tears
because he thought of Christmas Eve
in the Battle of the Bulge
where he was the one out of three survivors
of his company during World War II
and he would tell of how he
and his buddies found
a farmhouse on the outskirts
of Bastogne on Christmas Eve
and how they found a man and woman
and their children inside
and how the wife gave them
some soup and black bread
and how they stayed the night
and how somehow the farmhouse
was not hit as the war raged outside
and how they sang Christmas songs
that night with this Belgian family.
The words were different, he would say,
but the music was the same.

About the Author

Terry Allen was born in Brisbane, Australia in 1946. He was raised in Kansas City, Missouri and received his Ph.D. at Southern Illinois University in theatre arts. He is an emeritus professor at the University of Wisconsin-Eau Claire, where he taught acting, directing and playwriting. He is the author of the chapbook *Monsters in the Rain* (*Kelsay Books,* 2019) and his poems have appeared in numerous journals, including *Popshot Quarterly, Into the Void* and *Main Street Rag.* He lives in Columbia, Missouri with his wife Nancy and their dog Jayden.

Kelsay Books.com

www.ingramcontent.com/pod-product-compliance
Lightning Source LLC
LaVergne TN
LVHW050935080826
845145LV00004B/1278

* 9 7 8 1 9 5 4 3 5 3 1 0 7 *